To: _____

From _____

CHRIS SHEA

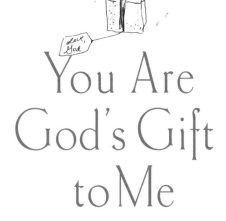

Love,
God

You Are
God's Gift
to Me

THOMAS NELSON
Since 1798

NASHVILLE   DALLAS   MEXICO CITY   RIO DE JANEIRO   BEIJING

Published by J. Countryman, a division of Thomas Nelson, Inc, Nashville,
Tennessee 37214.

Project manager: Terri Gibbs

Design: UDG | Designworks, Sisters, Oregon.

ISBN: 1-4041-0146-2

www.jcountryman.com
www.thomasnelson.com

Printed and bound in the United States of America

For Steve
My friend, my gift.

Every good gift
and every perfect
gift
is from above
and comes
down
from the Father
of
lights.
James 1:17

There is a wonderful
array of
gifts
in the world.

clocks and dolls,
   toasters,
Pearls,
   watches and
   bikes, goldfish
      and
beautiful
      bouquets
   of
      flowers.

But the best gift
I can think
of

is you,

you,
whose heart
is
tender

and
kind,

whose
smile
I
cherish
more

than the costliest
work of art.

You are
a gift
God
sent
to
me,

love,
God

a
happy blessing,
an
answered
prayer.

Of
this
I
have no
   doubt.

Because nothing but God's amazing grace

could account for the
joy of you
in my life.

Only the Father
of
lights
could send
such a treasure
as
You.

Where could you
come from, but the heart
of the One who is Love?

If only the
words existed
that would express
all you mean
to me...

Dictionary

← sorry!
not in
here...

...but no such words
have been
invented.

You add joy
to my
life,

It's true!

and color to

my

World ,

you really
do!

And
sometimes
just the
thought of you

makes me so happy I could cry.

Yours is the face...

... I can't
wait
to
see .

Yours is the laugh...

... I love to hear.

When the world feels cold,

thoughts of you make
it warmer.

And
When a day feels dark,

the sight of you makes it
brighter.

The One,

who sent

starlight

and

fireflies...

...sent
you
as well.

Planets!

Butterflies!

The moon shining
high in
the
sky!
You!....

All sent from
God and wrapped
up in His
Love.

Love,
God

(I happen
to think,

you were one
of
God's best
ideas . . . .)

You lift me up

when I'm feeling down,

and make me
laugh

when I'm
feeling blue;

When I'm with you,

I wish I could

keep the

sun from

setting...

so the
day
would
never
end.

Not a day goes
by,

not a single one

Thank you
Thank you
Thank you

that I don't give
God thanks...

for your dear heart,
your sweet face,
the sound of your
voice

and
your knock on
my door.

I thank Him
for the
good gift,
the perfect
gift,
sent from
up
above...

I thank Him
for
the
gift
of

you!